CHRIS, THE CLOUD MAKER

and OTHER POEMS

POEMS BY VEER SOROUT

Dedicating this book to my Family and Praniti, it would not have been possible without their support

FOREWORD

The onus of the maintenance of the world's soul lies not on the grizzled, veteran class of author alone: it lies upon also the wonder-eyed, creative youngsters who bring to the writing community a refreshing outlook.

Having had the pleasure of knowing Veer for a long time, I've found him to be an extremely creative boy with lots of fantasies and ambitions: to put it simply, he was a dreamer, and he still is, as you, the reader of his magnum opus, will soon find out. Being a creature who, perhaps, is not ignorant of the literary world and is enough of a panjandrum to call himself a part of it, when Veer asked me to write the foreword of this anthology, I was most honoured: because I'd personally found this task to be not only daunting, but something for which I myself was un-prepared. But, since I'd made a promise after all, I fired up my laptop, fixed myself a cup of coffee, downloaded Veer's work, and read it cover-to-cover: to the irrefutable conclusion that the boy had truly outdone himself, for he'd produced pieces of poet-ry that reflected the mindset of any other eleven-year old, but captured it so effectively and brilliantly that it had me at a loss of words for the better part of an hour.

Today, as I write this foreword, I will attempt to encroach upon some credit for the genius of this book by saying that once upon a time, I gave Veer a copy of Dahl's Danny, the Champion of the World. Why? For he's promulgated a compendium of poetry that would make the inventor of Gobble-funk proud: oh yes, we would all very much love to see our desktops grow legs, hack our very much despised teachers' computers, and stop them from sending any compromising emails to our parents to spare us a beating; we would also be ecstatic to see school cancelled when the world gets turned upside-down, I have no doubt! Again, Veer's writing, which is characterised by the innocence of his childhood, punctuated by his larger-than-life creative soul, and accentuated by his remarkable writing style transforms a collection of mere stanzas, four to five words per line, into something that will make readers not only enjoy it, but also wonder who this young lad from a seedy city in Haryana, India, is.

Ending this foreword, which to me seems to be a monumental task given my suspicions of the position that I have done Veer and his book justice, I can only say that the Chris, the Cloud Maker is a delectable read that will have a positive impact by all, who read it, irrespective of their age: the youngsters will enjoy it, the adults will be astonished by it, and book lovers like myself will be assured of the fact that the collective future of stories, poems, and all works that comprise the literary calendar is secure, with Veer and other children of his age ready to take the helm as and when the time arises.

Aditya Pratap Singh Phogat, A Reader

AUTHORS NOTE

I enjoyed creating this book with the support of my peers and mentor. They really helped by giving prompts and guiding me by making me add new vocabulary to the poems which you shall read later. They helped me create the titles and helped me procrastinate and clear my mind to write better. I just want to say that they have helped a lot.Despite meeting most of my peers recently, we have become the best of friends.The hours we spent sitting beside each other pointing out each other's mistakes will probably be the most memorable throughout my life unless something which is more fun, which will probably not happen. I have taken the time to write this author's note to appreciate my friends, family and most specially, You. I wrote this book to stand out and stand up to motivate all other students to try and discover their talent. Maybe it is mathematics, Or science— like my friend Jashn. Maybe it's English or Spanish, perhaps it is German. Or it's writing and poetry like me. I am writing this not for money but for competition, I want other children to compete with me or other writers.

INDEX

World Without Water

The Ballad Of The Watermelon

A Poetic Chorus About Chris, The Creator of Clouds

Eclipses And Myths

Sky–Earth Exchange Program

The Perfect Paradise

The Beauty of Fall

The Desktop With Feet

The World Without Nature's Beauty

The Square Sun

The Chalk with Life

The Way of The Dog's Nose

The Class of Skipping Classes

The School With no Teachers

The Cane of Terror

The Fastest Rabbit

The River of Coke

If A Piranha Was A Waiter In Starbucks

The Jaws That Ate Its Owner

WORLD WITHOUT WATER

The world without water

Water is

Cool and nice

But on the Earth

The water will be gone

No more clouds to

Block the summer sun

No more water for

Icy popsicles

All plants dead

No humans left

Only a camel is alive

Not looking for water

Just trying to survive

Plain dry land

No space for trees

Only boiling hot sand

Petrified logs

With no more dogs

Left to make happy

Only a plain red sky

Not even the buzzing of a fly

THE BALLAD OF WATERMELON

Red

Amber

Green

The colors of the Watermelon

Eternally on fire

In a situation so dire

It is getting hunted

By all the humans

No apple is helping

It just need quiet

As long as it has its powers

He will be forever running

From the humans

Alas its powers

The drinker of its juice

Shall be immortal

The gobbler of the fruit

Shall have superpowers

And the farmer of its seed shall

Gain great wealth

But the doers of these actions

Shall lead a

Cursed and wicked life

Their soul stuck in the void of the between

Forever they shall suffer in languish

A POETIC CHORUS ABOUT CHRIS, THE CREATOR OF CLOUDS

I always wonder

Who makes the clouds

For it is a task

For delicate hands

It must require a lot of time

But no one except the creator of clouds shall have

That much time

Sometimes it's a fluffy sheep

Others its a smooth horse

Sometimes they have to fill

The clouds with water

To save the Villages

In which the most devotees of god live

From the droughts of the season of summer

The creator of clouds

I shall name

After my pottery teacher

Whose name is Chris

Chris shall make a cloud

Oh watch it go by

Off to save the village

Full of devotees

But midway it encounters a plane

Who bursts the whole cloud

Causing it to burst

All the water flowing down

Makes the village flood up

Now the Sun shall come

And evaporate the water

Causing another drought but

Do not worry as Chris is here

ECLIPSES AND MYTHS

The moon blocks the sun

The sun tries to shine out of the edges

It succeeds for a minute but then the moon just comes back

People believe not to eat food

Or not to do work

Because of the eclipse

But it is really nothing

Its just the moon

Blocking the sun

People say don't eat meat

Or not to sleep

They say to shoot arrows at the sun

To shoo away the devil

Blocking the sun

In China they pray to the moon god

To make the devil go away

Somewhere in India

They say to fast

As to pray to god, To kill the devil

There are two types of eclipse

One with the moon where the moon glows red

The other is with the sun

Where the moon blocks the sun

Sometimes its fully

Others the sun

Just becomes a bright outline

You might think its dark

But it is actually very bright

You should not look at the eclipse

Without special glasses

Not many people are left

Full of superstitions

Only the grandmas and grandpas

Imagine these things.

SKY-EARTH EXCHANGE PROGRAM

The sky is over us

And the Earth under

But what if it was swapped

For a whole day

The shops would float around

The planes would crash in the new earth sky

As it is still solid

Lumberjacks would have no work

Neither would farmers

We would finally have flying cars

And school would be canceled

As it would be on the sky how would we be able to

Just get a plane ticket

For only a school

For it to crash up

In the sky

We would have the superpower

Of flight

Our pets could fly

My house will be able to hover

The crumbs of our bread

Wouldn't be able to get hoovered

The oxygen will be low

The pressure high

We would have to get

The tanks which

Divers use

Otherwise

We will die

The pressure in the sky

Will crush our lungs

But the oxygen bottles

Will help us survive

Boats will have to go around

Swimming in the empty sea

No more fish to catch

No more cows to milk

No more fruits to pluck

From their trees

Mucus will glide around

Disgusting everyone

THE PERFECT PARADISE

My dream place to live

Will be around the beach

On a remote island

With a Wifi tower

The house will be huge

And I will have a boat

To go fishing for food

I will grow a farm

And I will install a filter

To drink clean water

Soon I will be able to

Sustain myself

I will use the Mediterranean sun

To power my mansion

I will use wind turbines

And other sources of energy

I will buy a plane

To arrive at mainland

To pickup some meds

Or have fun with friends

Sometimes I will meet my parents

Others I will just be alone

And move around

Looking for fun

I would wash my own dishes

And clean my own clothes

Do my own work

And earn some of my own money

THE BEAUTY OF FALL

The Beauty of Fall

Is great

There are orange leaves

Crunchy leaves

And leaves which randomly fall on your head

Pumpkins are full in stock

So Starbucks makes Pumpkin Spice Latte

The surroundings are beautiful

And the euphony amazing

The weather is just perfect

Not cold

Not warm

It is not like summer

Neither like winter

It is its own season

It almost never rains

Protecting the plump pumpkins

Everything in fall is great

We get a school break

Monsoon is not very nice

Neither is summer

The only great seasons are

Spring and Fall

THE DESKTOP WITH FEET

My desktop grew feet overnight

Now it is begging me to go to school with him

I will take it on one condition

It silences the teacher from reading

And lets us have fun

When it is math

The desktop

Will give me answers

And when it is PE

It will let us watch a video

At lunch it will order

A burger for everyone

Except all the teachers

If the principal mails our parents

It will hack the computer

And stop all mails

Protecting everyone, from a bad beating

STYLISH RINGS FROM SATURN

I wear Saturn's rings

On my fingers

They feel very rough

As they are made

Out of rocks

And a lot of dust

I go to the scientists lab

And show my rings

Which help them learn

More about Saturn

When i'm not at the scientists

I wear them for

Style

People say they look

Cool

And I greatly agree with them

When it's time to sleep

They go into my cupboard

With the biggest lock

So no one will steal them

Now it's time for me to doze off

And step into a dream

A WORLD WITHOUT NATURE'S BEAUTY

A world without

Flowers will be

Empty and ugly

All flowers are beautiful

And serve their own purposes

I can't make my tea

Without hibiscus flowers

You can't scent your house

Without a rose or dandelion

And people won't be able to digest

Without their dose of daisy

The world will be robbed of its beauty

And all its fragrant

Smells

Trees will be empty

And fruits won't be able to grow

As buds turn into flowers

But flowers aren't there

Medicine gone

Coffee gone

Only plain grass left

THE SQUARE SUN

If I could

Change the shape

Of the sun

It would be into a square

The sun would follow

The Earth's face

Light would be a plain unbendable line

Solar eclipses would be

More interesting

As the square

Would outline the circle

I would maybe see the sun

For what it truly is

But the others might

Not see even half the truth

THE CHALK WITH LIFE

I once met a chalk

Which had a soul

It could write itself

And make a lion move

Despite it not being alive

It expressed itself

Through making drawings

And writing words

It could make the most realistic flower

Or the most cartoony dog

It would cross out math from the board

And convert Spanish to English

Oh the fun we had

And the boards we crossed out

The teachers were so livid

As they had been working for hours

The timetable would say it is dispersal right now

Or school never started

Now the chalk started to run out

So we captured its soul

And put it into another chalk

The chalk never died

As long as I was there

As I would just transfer the soul

Before it ran out

ALL ABOUT THE DOG'S NOSE

I am a dog

And my nose is my strongest tool

With it I can find out

If you have ever petted

Any other dog

You have to take me everywhere you go

Or I will whine all day

Even while you sleep

My nose can find

Any treats you hid

Even if its on the other side of the house

It is not hidden from me

I will protect you from the paper and packages

And the hoover which sucks my fur

Or even the occasional neighbor

In return I ask you for

Treats, water and a scratch on my fur

I don't like water

So don't make me bathe

Or I will whimper all day

My bark can wake the whole street

Maybe even the town

But that's just my habit

Because I am just a dog

THE CLASS OF SKIPPING CLASSES

There is this one class

Which everyone loves

Only the teachers pet hates it

It's called Skip A Class 101

You can learn to skip class

And get away with it

The teacher gave one homework

Skip the class once a week

And give the best excuse

The best excuse will win

The teachers being their servant

For a whole day

You can command them to massage your legs

Or you can make them order you a pizza

You can choose your work

You can choose your seat

You can choose everything

Including your absence or presence

This is the best class

No one can hate it unless

They are the teachers pet

THE SCHOOL WITH NO TEACHERS

There is this school

With absolutely no teachers

The students just come

And do whatever the want to

They play games till

School hours end

They can get their phone out in the class

They can use their laptop to watch videos

They can order lasagnas for lunch

And burritos for breakfast

The teachers don't come

But they still get paid

I do not know how

The school is still running

Some weeks the children

Come during the weekend

Or even the holidays

The mayhem which is created

Is too powerful

You can even hear

It from the other side of the world

That is the reason

Why no teacher comes

THE CANE OF TERROR

Inspired by Matilda's Miss Trunchbull

Oh, the Cane

Of the principal

Absolutely bias and

Propagate and thin

I do not know

A single young boy

Who would not be scared

Of the Cane of Terrors

It is used on the one

Who forgets their homework

Or the one who does dirty work

The Cane is a holy terror

Made by the cruelest of inventors

It was solely made

To beat the little children

It is quick and rigid

The precision more accurate

Than a sniper

It will leave your bottom aching

For the rest of the day

THE FASTEST RABBIT

I met a rabbit

So quick and agile

That it can create a F5 tornado

It can make a hurricane

And run through buildings

It can run on the walls

It can travel a thousand miles

Just in a blink of the eye

It did not drink water

But it drank Red Bull

From cans left beside the toll

It does not eat carrots

It eats the energy bars

Left inside the door of cars

It is fast

Faster than a

F1 car

It will beat all in a race

Even the fastest car

It will make your head spin

It will make you dizzy

It can make you go crazy

Upon seeing its speed

You will not plant a single seed

Of Junk Food

THE RIVER OF COKE

There once was a river

Not full of water

But thousands of gallons

Of flowing Coke

The village next to it

Never had worries

For all they could worry

Coke would wash it away

They didn't have normal dough

Their dough was slightly sweet

As it was not made of water

But a handful of Coke

The lemonade

Which they made

Was just lemony Coke

The river was brown and not clear

The liquid never had to be filtered

As it was already clean

No germs

No dirt

Only tasty fresh Coke

Only once was it expired

Causing a humongous plague

Which was cured by

Drinking a glass of water

For water is the only liquid

Which cannot be expired

Doesn't matter if its from Mount Fuji

Or even the River Ganges

It will never be expired

Unless it has dirt in it

IF A PIRANHA WAS A WAITER IN STARBUCKS

In the bustling cafe,

A waiter stalks the floors

Not in an apron

But in scales which shimmer and soar

With a grin as sharp as teeth

And eyes as keen as knives

This piranha serves tables

And changes our lives

Swift and agile,

Weaving through the crowd

Balancing trays of dreams

Never a shroud

Orders taken in a flash

With a flick of his tail

Ensuring each diners story

Like a well-told tale

In the chaos of clinking and chatter

This waiter-piranha navigates

Nothing the matter

A whisper of water

In each elegant stride

Carrying wishes and laughter,

Nowhere to hide

The expertise not in pen and notepad, no

But in the dance of service,

Where wishes flow

From Java - Chip

To lava-hot dips

Each bite watched by gleaming, cheery eyes

No need for words when a glance conveys

The promise of another round

And the chefs praise

In the depths of the dining sea
They excel

The piranha-waiter

Where service casts it spell

So raise a glass to this unique blend

Of predators and service

Where legends mix

For in this cafe of tales

Where moments entwine

The piranha-waiter ensures your feast will be divine.

Finally, you have reached the end. It does not matter what your age is, for you have persevered through all the poems. Now, it is time for my favourite poem "Jaws That Ate Is Owner"

THE JAWS THAT ATE ITS OWNER

Humans create smoke

Humans create plastic

They litter the Earth endlessly

And cut trees all day

They consume Mother Earth's resources

And ruin her land

Now dogs and cats

Have no place to live

Except the humans homes

They eat the dogs and cats prey

And feed them shaped wheat

Humans protect Earth for a day

On so called World Environment Day

And go back to their antics the next

They eat veggies for a day

And then back to their meat

Who will protect humans

From their own, consuming Jaws?